May the Generations Die in the Right Order

poems by

Penelope Scambly Schott

MAIN STREET RAG PUBLISHING COMPANY
CHARLOTTE, NORTH CAROLINA

Cover art by: Penelope Scambly Schott

Acknowledgements:

Calyx, "The Purpose of Purpose"
Chance of a Ghost, "May the Generations Die in the Right Order"
Cider Press Review, "Opal Creek, or the Engines", "What I Learned about Fish Today"
Comstock Review, "December Again," "Cleopatra's Parents Were Brother and Sister"
Footwork, "Dancing on the Berlin Wall"
Georgetown Review, "At the Open Air Concert with my Sister
Georgia Review, "In this time of war"
Grove Review, "Drowned Twin"
Journal of Feminist Studies in Religion, "Caring for the World"
Louisiana English Journal, "The Angels of New Orleans"
New Verse News, "The Angels of New Orleans" (on-line)
No Tell Motel, "Duenna"
Passager, "One Theory of Composition"
Phi Kappa Phi Forum, "The Ladylike Cough"
Santa Cruz/ Monterey Branch of NWU, "Flying East for my Grandson's Birth" (1st prize)
Tiger's Eye, "Prelude to a *memento-mori*", "Everybody Here Loves Dogs", "I Am your Dead Dog", "Somewhere to Sleep", "Transaction", "What's the Matter in my Marriage Now"
U.S. 1 Worksheets, "Blue Schooner', "Several Short Questions about Crumbs"
Voice Catcher, "What's Inside"

Library of Congress Control Number: 2007933191

ISBN: 978-1-59948-062-6
ISBN: 1-59948-062-X

Produced in the United States of America

Main Street Rag
PO Box 690100
Charlotte, NC 28227-7001
www.MainStreetRag.com

in memory of Sadie Schott Sweetdog

CONTENTS

1. The Art of Dying

2. The Art of Living

3. The Art of Love

4. The Spirit of the World

1. The Art of Dying

What's Inside

When I opened the box
and took out the bag

when I unfolded the top of the bag
and reached in past my wrist

when I unfurled my fingers
and poked toward the bottom of the bag

when I stroked something
that almost felt like fur

it was my dead father's springy white hair
it was my yellow dog's silky coat

it was the channeled mink coat of the lady
who used to live downstairs

it was the silk-lined ermine muff
from when I was a princess

it was the damp taste of my yellow pigtail
wound around a puffy red thumb

it was one howl in a chorus
on this treeless hill

it was the tufted and variegated pelt
I am sprouting in my sleep

Prelude to a *memento-mori*

1. Ceremony

I am streaking my cheeks
with fresh mud;

when I enter the earth,
I shall be greeted.

2. Old dog

Her feathered legs twitch on the mat
and I ask, *What are you dreaming?*

Each morning her fur is still breathing.
I know because I check.

My last desire:
somebody stir my ashes with hers.

3. Where I've been

I made a baby
who made a baby

who made a song
while standing within

the sleeping spindles
of his crib, crooning,

Ma-ma-ma-ma, soon,
inside the darkened room.

4. Darkness

Spaces among the Pleiades,
the music of rot in the icebox,

or the way I knelt in my petticoat
between humped rows

to dig under stones for tender potatoes:
this is my list about darkness.

I am going there slowly, but I keep
to the trail.

My address book is full
of dead people.

Tonight when I phone them,
will a bell sound in my house?

What the Bed Knows

I am a bed in a busy house of loss,
frost in the yard and inside the house.

Today I am married to the lamp shade:
we cast our hot eye on the damp head

of a solitary woman dreaming of lions,
whiskers purring, fur on the quilt, not

this wide, cold sheet. No silence
ever wider than death, no absence

more complete. The languor of grief
astounds her. Her fingers are weak,

and she holds sadness like a handful
of loose gravel,

not knowing how to set it down.

The Final Extinction of Ceremony

Someone was coming like wind in the pines–
a procession of she-goats, each with a bell
hanging down from her beard.

Someone was shoveling humus into a hole–
an ossuary of pots, each with its green spring
shrinking to snowcrust.

Now someone chants from a dark mouth–
somebody bites off the stems of the bells,
each cup spilling

its ultimate note; and now someone swallows
the iron clappers.

Granddaddy's Shovel with a Chipped Blue Handle

– in memory of H.G. 1922-1944

As if blue
As if ageing blue veins at the dish of my ankle

or my baby sister's blue lips on the shore of Lake Michigan
in the green summers of primary school

As if blue twilight over the playground
and the blue-gray chains of the grown-up swings

yielding and tightening, rising
toward the grouted red brick of the school house

and swinging backwards so that the brittle
yellow and black telegram is always not yet arriving

and my tall uncle in the Merchant Marine still grins
on the deck just like he grinned in the snapshot

and my grandfather stokes the blue flame in the coal furnace
as if we will always be warm

as if as yet he knows only one good thing
to do with a shovel

May the Generations Die in the Right Order

When hemlock branches fold down
like the ribs of an old umbrella,

when wet midnight skips in the gutter,
spluttering down the rain chain,

you, there, old lady,
WAKE UP.

A dream summons: flare of sheeting.
Stand on this square of street light.

Hold out your arms like twin
perches for songbirds. Now trill.

Keep on trilling. Let the pitch rise.

Your grown children will tell you
when you may sleep again.

See.
They are floating toward you

with sharp umbrellas.
Arriving with hot eyes.

Several Short Questions about Crumbs

Remember Woody Allen not doing his homework
because in a few billion years our sun will burn out?

How could we make it until tomorrow without denial?
Entropy being the natural state, why sweep the floor?

Just for the whisper of bristles moving over lumber?
To mark before and after dinner? For the spell

of my long skirt twirling? Who believes the world
applies to them? *Dying*, I mean.

So I keep on sweeping.
But why?

For the cockeyed dance of the red-painted handle?
Or simply to delight the straw?

Drowned Twin

His wish
was to lift his green stone hands.

He had rested his face
on the river bottom

where lullabies for minnows
couldn't help.

I knew what would happen:
Spring-rising is a fact

we learned when his bones
surfaced in the lower meadow.

Such certainty comforts our father
while our mother sighs over her son

in his wedding suit of lupine.
Now I carry his death

like a blue bouquet,
like a promise encrypted

in clear water,
like a second heart in my chest.

Two Elements

1

Scabbed crab apple logs flaming
in the fireplace, the hissing cinders.

Joan of Arc and her heretic horse,
the debridement of roasted skin,

or the sweet fat in a baby, rendered,
like fat in a goose. A sizzle and shrink

of torched ants. In the big black kettle,
beribboned generals boil blood soup.

Daddy's long bones chill in an urn.
When Crow snatched fire out

of the sun, it was a boy's prank.

2

Watch any woman walk under rain:
small runnels collect and puddle

in the bare troughs of her shoulders.
She enters the dark kitchen, cool

in her washed flesh. Inside the house
of the roasted seed, I am small

and angular and mud green
and I lie on the tongue of my lover

until his lips buzz with an icy tingle
like mint or wintergreen or crab apple,

each leaf inscribed with one message:

> *bud and green, yellow and fallen,*
> *burnt and gone.* Cold crab apple ash.

2. The Art of Living

Everybody Here Loves Dogs

The men in this village have wide shoulders
with thick tendons to sustain a left wing
Around the blacksmith's black forge
each man is beating his one wing
until sparks mix with the stars

The dogs in our village
carry willow baskets in their white teeth
They trot from hut to hut to offer us apples
They also bring crying human babies
to milky human breasts

Each woman in my village
has a sequined right wing
whose glitter echoes the stars
Our wings sing about moonlight
while the moon holds its white breath

Now the blacksmith abandons his forge
Each dog curls into three circles
and the babies bubble from pursed lips
Matched pairs of women and men
hold hands beneath their opposite wings

I will dwell in our village forever
in the deep shelter of mountains
I will walk among fir trees
With the sequined tip of my wing
I will scribble peace on the fog

So here's what I think I know:
that these are the wings of the village:
fir trees and the sharp mountains
Imagine, you villagers, the elastic wings
of the flightless human heart

Transaction

Drink the world.
Hold the fog in your pink mouth.

My dog has lovely black lips.
The curl of her tongue ladles water

from a blue bowl, her ribs rising
into morning, unlike my old father

dead in his sleep, the last breath
seeping from his lungs,

those long transactions of in-and-out
completed.
                    Come. Can you picture

the damp thoroughfares of the body
like flowering April boulevards

crowded with celebrants, and all of us,
each one, here at the granite curb,

applauding, applauding, applauding,
applauding like madwomen?

My Change of Occupation

–for my grown children

1.

I live in terror of two things, Death and Life.

My white-haired mother-in-law was dying.
Her six gray-haired children sat up all night
at the foot of their sick mother's bed,

and I was sore afraid.

I was afraid that nobody would ever love me
that much; I was afraid of putting anybody
to that much trouble.

Which only partly explains
why all day long I kept on stepping,

right foot
directly in front of
left foot,

along the eroded narrow edge
of the cliff. Below me,

the river

lurched over
rocks.

2.

I live in terror of two things, Height and Crevice.

Trapped beneath boulders,
                                        one small stone
beat itself smooth in the current until

it was hard as a clenched fist,
tight as a contracted heart.

3.

I live in terror of two things, Him and Her.

I would proffer to my son
I would proffer to my daughter

my stone heart to eat for dessert
but I can't cut it   in halves.

Whichever one of the two of them
swallows it
                    whole
will choke,
choke.

4.

Back in our former life I was a used sponge
soaking up fury and want. I lived in the middle
of a steamy kitchen. Don't you both remember?

So late, my grown-up darlings, forgive me:

> *whenever I needed to feed you,*
> *I squeezed myself dry*
> *into the thin*
> *soup.*

5.

Children, spit me back into the river;
help me become a River Stone.

Now tell me, how do you fancy
my change of occupation?

The Geology of Flesh

I used to remember hanging from trees,
how I nested in crotches of branches,
how cool leaves exhale in the dark.

I liked the firelight inside the cave
where all my dances were magnified,
how the clefts in the rock spoke.

I knew that the center of life
was the slit in the living flesh
where one body links to another.

I will poke my fingertips into holes
in rocks where small crustaceans
died in the salt sea

before the limestone silted down,
before the layers bent themselves
around white fossils in highway cuts,

before I sat in a crowded room
and didn't know where to put
my cunning hands. Only the babies

remember:

look how they suck on their thumbs,
those little hairless thumbs,
so pink and plump, so damp.

Hard Sweeping

The frazzled straw of my broom bends to the right;
must I always sweep in the same direction?

> A woman with a broom
> is a shaker of cradles;
> she tortures her children
> by sweeping in riddles.

My elegant mother never swept her own floor;
shall I pay a stranger to dance with my broom?

> A woman with a broom
> is a woman possessed;
> she pirouettes with demons
> who hang from her breasts.

There is dried mud on the floor of the cave;
is it pocked with the footprints of midnight rats?

> A woman with a broom
> is the enemy of worms;
> she sweeps out the dead
> into underground rooms.

I am stepping over my mother's bones;
shall I hack off my hair with a sharp flint?

> A woman with no broom
> attaches her hair
> with rat sinew
> to her mother's femur.

Now I crouch forward to sweep the floor;
the claws of my toes carve spirals in rock.

My black tongue licks grooves in the dark.

Possessing the Galaxy

When I was eight I made a planetarium
with rolled black paper and a flashlight.

We lived on the thirteenth floor with a high
bathroom window where a yellow canary

flew in and then out and a praying mantis
spread its legs on the closed lid of the toilet.

When I heard a joke about a man's thingie,
that was the first toilet that came to mind.

I am always memorizing the tile squares
in front of that tall toilet. If I rang the bell

at 915 West End Avenue, apartment 13A,
I wouldn't need to go in to remember.

Although the canary has lifted me away,
decades lie below me like tiny tiles.

When I get so old that I forget my words
and my husband and my children,

I will still be eight in my white gloves,
cotton gloves that came to my wrists.

The narrow wrists. The white hands.
Drawing my map of the tile cracks.

At the Open Air Concert with my Sister

–for Heather

On the far side of the lawn, the music is blowing away;
I want to wrap a cirrus cloud over my sister's gray hair.

She sits on a plaid blanket like a baby about to topple;
I want to rub lotion of linden into her cracked heels.

Twilight blackens the grass. Here at the curtain of dark,
strangers with paper cups are swallowing their losses.

Our past is another time zone: a frayed satin ribbon
draped in the cookbook marks my sister's birthday cake.

Did I bake it and ice it and spell out her name in sugar?
We used to play on the floor. I did *this little piggy*

on her hands and her round toes. *Whee, whee, whee,*
all the way home. Each high note floating away.

Once, when I got home from first grade, my sister
was waiting on the sidewalk in a brown felt hat

with a brown grosgrain ribbon. She had become
a personage instead of a thing, and, for the first time

ever, I shaped in my mind that plain word *love.*
I felt air dividing our two breathing mouths.

Two roller skates and four feet so we held hands –
the break in the sidewalk got sticky and red.

On a night like this night in a town like any town,
the chance of disease or despair or a random gun.

Black spot mildew kissing the rose. I will entomb
her cheekbones under the bones of my face.

My sister and I crawled under the porch. We peeked
out through cracked lattice. Green and blue glass

and the rubble of old concrete dented our scabby knees.
It was our house or a boat or a Gothic cathedral

and all afternoon we lived there for our whole lives
until somebody rang a bell.

Always that bell, even while I was forgetting to listen.
Last dinner with my father. Green beans and fish.

Until early the following morning we still had a daddy.
The book he'd been reading, bookmark neatly in place.

Everything I read before his bookmark, he and I shared.
But after the bookmark. My sister and I both living

in the always after. Dark music over the lawn. I twist
one finger through her gray ringlets. How it keeps on

starting and stopping.

The Chairs

If I leave my house and return too soon,
I discover the chairs conversing in a circle

They say, *she left* or *he came back*
or *noontide* or *summer*

They hold the hand prints of babies
learning to circumnavigate the room

My dead father sits on the brown leather chair
nodding his clever chin

How like him to sneak back on me,
how like him this half-smile, lifting the corners

of his bottom lip

When I ask him what I should do, he tells me,
never slam shut a door

He tells me, *every atom of every chair is busy*
being itself

If I look down at my hands, each open palm
is singing with minutes

When I toss the minutes up in the air, they fall
in front of me and behind

Daddy, you make me giggle; you make me
want to start tickling

the implacable back of every chair

Use Caution When Taking the Bull by the Horns

Wear leather gloves, thick skin, a scrim of gorgeous
ignorance.

Call for the bandilleros and the picadors.
Call for the doctor, call for the nurse,
call for the lady with the alligator purse.

You know, I knew that lady. She used to visit my mother.
The furs at her neck bit each other's tails.

It was dangerous back in 1949:
the Italians were still starving, and warehouses by the Thames
were soot black. My little sister almost died
because her throat was too small.

All my life I have listened for breathing.
When I am lucky, I can feel the earth inhale,
grasses rising like the messy coat
of a very old dog.

Who will listen for breaths when I am gone?
Who listened before I was born?

I must take the bull by the horns and leap onto
his humped back. We will chase that cow
over fresh moons.

Olly-olly-in-come-free.

Mother, I am hiding under the washtub.
Daddy, I am hiding under the lilacs.
I am holding my breath. Anyone here,
come find me.

I have been hiding for fifty years.

Console Me

The white-faced cattle turning aside
their wide heads–

the afternoons are long catastrophes,
each sunset breakable.

Behind white railings of porches,
shadows fracture;

no one descends the steps.

All night,
during and during and during,

my cheek wrinkles
on a cool pillowcase.

The peace of pain: to expect nothing
and get it,

until all I recall about comfort

is a flock of birds
on the one flat spot in the ocean.

What I Learned about Fish Today

The physical grief of the hatchery fish harrows me:
the dorsal fin just visible before the flying rise and
thunk on the slanted metal barricade, the slide
back. The lacerated flesh. To have come so long
from the sea for this, to have been thus deceived–
does the black jaw of the chinook quiver before
the flat eye fades?

Here I could do the poetic leap and return to
what made me: to travel for years in a worldly
sea, before the one bay, one river, one tributary,
the one home creek; my daddy's pipe tobacco,
roast beef and soap in a grandmother's kitchen,
the boy whose knitted hat I stole and buried
under my pillow to sniff, what calls us back.

Yet the salmon seems to believe it is going forward
and maybe it is, up the fish ladder into the trap, into
the hatchery of manufactured currents and tanks,
knives and buckets to cull and mix the eggs and milt.
The fisherman I saw today had half a face, burn scars
where one ear should be, one eyelid scanty and tight.
And though what has happened to me

is less visible than what has happened to him
and even fishing is a damned bloody business,
the man with half a face loved the fish he pulled
from the river. It lay in a galvanized tub on top
of a Butterfingers wrapper, and he would rinse, gut
and cook it, and it would taste sweet as spun sugar
in the undamaged cave of his twisted mouth.

The Purpose of Purpose

All day yesterday I thought about salmon,
their stolid determination,

but when I woke up this morning
hearing the creek, I thought

joy, maybe it's *joy*,
the way sunshine pulls me

or harmonica music
or the thick forest across the creek,

my bare feet on the wide pine boards
or a dry leaf falling onto water–

the whole flowing skin of the world
like the re-discovered skin of a lover,

like the tips of my thumb and forefinger
touching

in order to circle
blue zero in the sky.

Here is the circle

touching the circles like complicated gears
unlocking the tumblers of the great vault
of the night where every deed is recorded
on the pale whirls of your ten fingertips
or in fairy circles of mushroom spores:
that delicate flesh and those lilting feet
of all your children who never sprang up
to be born.

Chinoiserie

My hand is mottled and scabbed like this shattered
green bottle scattered by the front step of a plundered
farm house down at the end of a dirt road. It hurts
to empty the mailbox of yellowed flyers for auctions
of tractors and tires and blades to obsolete machinery.

Chinoiserie from the mantle is now for sale in a shop in
a town where I'll never stop–not even for coffee or gas–
and this last red tulip I tear by the broken step, a token
of someone who cared once for beauty, is leaking sap
from its torn stem.

Why speak of a hard hand sweeping ruins, gathering
shards? I always bend to the faded places–their grace,
the way they don't end–

Opal Creek, or the Engines

1

Invisible among moving currents,
fins ripple in a grotto of rocks.

Sucking at moss in the waterfall,
mouth as round as lidless eyes.

In the braided tresses of water,
fish scales and stamped iron.

When last I swam here,
I had different fingers,

until I swam up
through the opal rooms.

2

When I flew to Resolute Island
with the ex-love of my life,

we were mere miles
from the magnetic North Pole

and copulated in a Quonset hut.
Now the news never surprises me:

it seems that magnetic North
is gradually moving west.

On frozen Resolute Island
they never shut off the engines.

3

I'm always searching for what I've lost:
some hard object that served a function;

not a crochet hook or a nutmeg grater,
surely not a Philips head screwdriver.

I recall only how it lay on my hand,
how solid, how resolutely it glittered.

Here on the river bottom,
even if I am sedimentary,

the skinny red needle of
the missing compass will

still be quivering.

3. The Art of Love

High masts are rocking

starboard to port, those twin portals
for dreams of leaving and coming back

as the wide sea rides in on the moon
to shed crabs at wrack-line,

that quick skitter over whitecaps
basking in fire, and a black shadow

slashing the sun. A woman I know,
raw with divorce and raving about loons,

insists: *to court or to migrate*
            is one same song.

But that is not my song.
I am the one who has raked my youth

into bonfires, like the stammering dialects
of beacons. Peace, peace,

the broad arms of the jetty,
and all the mended nets.

Places of Refuge

The swale of scarf on the grand piano,
the woven golden tassel hanging down from the lamp,
an empty paper bag when the cat scoots out, the dark place
where my shoes hold the shapes of my toes.

I found a place inside your cheek where my tongue just fits,
I found a place in the curled fist of an infant where my thumb
is a giant who will never swallow me up.

This world is dangerous and large:
Thumbelina on your lilypad, carry your treasure
in the husk of a magic bean, chimes of an ice cream truck
ringing a white fugue around the blue lake.

I will carve my grave with a silver butter knife,
I will decorate the sides with white roots and tunnels of worms.

Long ago it was summer and all of us beautiful on the lawn.
Olly-olly-in-come-free: to have been, to be, to be and be
the last child hidden too well in the cellar, thin centipedes
scattering like playmates under the bulkhead doors,
the dim evening, and everyone else gone home.

Guardian

Once, in my childhood, my girlfriend and I
sprawled on the painted sand.

We lay like lovers on the heat of a rock;
we warmed like snakes on a May afternoon.

We contained so much longing that our ribs
sprang open, exploding to breasts.

We became one woman with four breasts;
we were surprised and also not surprised.

To say we contained the round earth is
to say too little.
Now

a woman with four breasts summons
the rain to come down and suckle.

Come down, she moans, *all of my breasts*
are burning.

Her milk is the venom and the anti-venom.
It flows between layers of shale.

This four-breasted woman promises,

You may bury your mother and father
safely

inside our own wet planet.

The Blue Schooner

1. The Voyage Out

A broom sweeping my hopes away, or the way
he shot buckshot right through the rusted screen
into the musty front room. And whom can I ask
why he did it? Whom can I ask why I stayed?

A blue schooner is cruising the spume of the sea.
On board, our crew of foolish brides clambers
up the rigging on the tilted mast, riding swells
and troughs, the swing of our lanterns green

with bullet glass, red with embers. Below deck,
our babies are howling. There is no breast
sweet enough or full to staunch their hunger.
Why linger on this old story? Did you expect

enlightenment? No. I am reefing sails, coiling
rope. A dangerous voyage and decades long.
Until I crouch again in that front room, buckshot
rolling under the floral couch. I was so loyal

to him for so long. So long.
And oh, my shipmates, so far
to sail home.

2. At the Edge

When I was twenty, I ran away from my parents,
my chances, my high grades, into the raw kitchen
of marriage, whoever he was, convenient.

Now I have traded beauties–my lithe young waist
for the handles of paintbrushes: *alizarin crimson,*
hansa yellow, ultramarine.

When I was twenty, I reckoned with equations;
I danced like Kali with dozens of arms and legs
under the tinseled basketball nets.

Safely sixty, I count in wet laps of the crawl.
I swam to the lost edge where finned monsters
invited me in. I still hear them.

I also hear tides roll over the globe, the old
people breathing by choice, the tired dogs, eyes
speaking pain as if they believe I should know

what to do. At twenty I knew how to breed,
to grow fat babies and push them into the light;
now I see pattern, light and dark, lilacs

coming back and back, the fleshy perfume
of lilacs, their immortal taste.

3. Credo

The whale who walked
on the flowerless land
has come down to saltwater.

I went to the sea with a shovel,
I went to the ocean with a pail,
I stepped in the blood

between islands,
I learned the specific gravity of trouble,
I studied new ways to fail.

Inside their slick flippers, the seals
have eloquent hands. They signal
their songs in the long lines of the tide.

Here on the wracked beach,
I am caught in the damp wings of the sea,
rapt and blind,

wrapped in those wings of disbelief,
such vast appendages, those wet
electric engines of the mind.

Ex-husband

I hadn't understood my breath
until that long ago Friday night you tried

to choke me,

until tremulous lungs, wanting the whole sky,
burned in my chest.

Whatever you've strangled past shaping
into words will still be true.

You are not the first in the line of drunken men
whose silence smoulders in their hands. I keep

in my lap a small olive wood bowl containing
all the air in the world. The bowl began

as an ancient tree in a white landscape
where silver roots slithered under cliffs,

the shape of its twisting visible as tendons,
its slenderest twigs bendable as cartilage,

and the wood, when polished by hands, smooth
as the bruised skin at the base of my throat.

Back when you did it, I was so ashamed
of my fear, my breasts, my need to breathe,

that years later, I am still collecting my words
like rainwater into this bowl.

Rose for an Ex-lover

I give you the tips of the thorns
in the pads of your cow-handed fingers,
I give you the sparse sap
for your guzzling mouth,
I give you the tight green petals
that circle the rose hip,
I give you the faithful man in the rose garden
plying his clippers and rake,
I give you the tin bucket
where slit stems drown.

If ever you gave me a rose,
I don't remember it;
if you promised tomorrow,
I don't remember that either.
I don't even recall why I loved you.
If you cast more than a small shadow
in a cut field at the height of noon,
I didn't see it.

I remember grasping the wing of a gray moth,
I remember the powder that stuck on my two fingers,
I remember how much it tasted of nothing.

With you and me,

there were always limits. I was pregnant so briefly
before I cramped and bled.

For one evening we planned our wedding; for one afternoon
I shopped for a dress.

Then came a morning like many mornings when you wanted
to screw and we did,

and you got out of bed and left, and I knew we were done.

Now, decades later, you are less permanent than the woman
I glimpsed from a London train.

Again, it was morning. Her face lit up the window square
in a grid of window squares

in a maze of council housing, and the curly tips of her hair,
red-blond and wild, touched the edges

of the casement, and I wanted to leap from the train and run
back to her stark building

and ring every buzzer until I found her, because I knew
if I found her,

there would be no limits.

The Last Thirst

A woman in a gray veil entered the cave. She lifted a bucket. The dim shadow of her bucket moved on the wall.

Silver tree roots twisted down through rock. The gray woman didn't know whether the tree was alive above the cave.

She didn't know about the snake hanging from the highest branch of the tree or the light of the evening star as it glittered on the lacquered scales of the snake.

She held her bucket under the cleft in the rock. Water gathered and fell.

Each drop rose up like a nipple in the skin of water at the bottom of the bucket before it went flat.

I have been thirsty a long time. My breasts are empty and my children old.

Now I am swallowing the water and the snake and the whole evening star. Soon I will be sucking on the silver roots of the tree.

Tonight I will lie down to sleep on the cool floor of the cave.

I will rest my veiled head on the crook of my arm. Starlight will shine from inside my skin. Each crease in my flesh will gleam.

The Velvet Peaches of August

When stars rise over the mountain,
fruit gleams in the half-picked orchard.

As I wait for you among velvet peaches,
I stand in darkness on their bruised flesh.

Sweetness. Sweetness gathers like bees
at the mouth of juice. I meant to want you,

yes, but never this much.

Years

As I watch this blanket rise and sink over my husband's
sleeping shoulder, I remember an orange salamander
lying across my palm, its skin like slubbed silk but elastic
and more delicate, the damp bellows of its lungs flaring
inside its chest, its soft sides expanding and deflating,
its orange breath brushing my hand like our sun itself,
pulsing.

And now, at breakfast, as I place the smooth tip
of his index finger against the cheek of this ripe apricot,
a skim of light ignites the curly hairs above his knuckles–
years, and my face hugged between his two palms like
the muzzle of the dog we've loved beyond speaking of.

What's the Matter in my Marriage Now

The old dog sleeps under a chair,
silver muzzle on crossed paws.
The room collects itself around her.

A man with a gray beard
and a woman with pale hair
walk in slow circles around the chair.

Good dog, he says, walking clockwise.
Poor old dog, says she, counterclockwise.
The dog opens her filmy brown eyes.

The man offers the dog a beef treat
which the dog accepts gently
but must be coaxed to eat.

The woman casts herself onto the rug.
She slides part way under the chair.
She hugs the dog into her belly.

The man's feet back away from the shadow
of the chair. *Good dog, good dog, good dog*,
he repeats and repeats and repeats,

while the woman keeps licking the dog's fur.
This woman, this woman who is almost old,
is choking on grief.

Duenna

This is the double bed
these are the dented pillows
this is the family dog
her yellow fur on the cotton sheets
her yellow fur on the crimson quilt

Fur on skin and skin on skin
slow wakings of a Saturday morning
rain on the tall windows
rain in the dark limbs of the firs
bamboo wind chime singing of rain

This is the double bed
these are the arms and legs
these are the lips touching the lips
and this is the yellow dog
unwilling to go out in the rain

Legs around legs and tongue to tongue
such heat beneath the crimson quilt
and oh, the old yellow bitch
who will ignore almost anything
just to stay here in our bed

Nothing surprises an old dog
Douglas firs rising into fog
winter rain sluicing the panes
wooden clang of the wind chime
the rock-rock-rocking of the bed

She and I have squatted in woods
and slept off fevers on long afternoons
so now I am floating somewhere else
and it's just my very busy husband
whom the dog stares flat in the eye

You Could Call This *Contentment*

When my 3rd husband promised to be faithful
until death do us part, I was glad we had both
slept around.

I am no longer curious
re: the slant of the member, hang of the balls,
the texture of hair in the pubes.

I am not particularly intrigued
by exclamations, ejaculations,
or post-coital snores.

I am more interested
in the flat width of his thumb
pressing my palm under the sheet.

Some nights I watch him by starlight,
some nights he saves me from drowning.
The only part I dislike in this story

is death will us part.

Give me the tale of oatmeal in the morning,
maybe with cranberries,
and scanning the Sunday ads.

As for all those men on the planet
who may remember my hips,
whose mouths have tasted my flesh,

some of them are eating oatmeal,
some are reading the sports section;
I hope their team won.

I hope their favorite player
has popped up out of the huddle
to carry the ball home.

Cleopatra's Parents Were Brother and Sister

In the wake of her barge, ripples
of disappointment burnished the Nile.

Poor Marc Antony never had a chance;
Cleopatra couldn't love him like her parents

might have loved one another:

> to think the same word at the same time,
> taste an equal sweetness of palm wine,
>
> trace a perfect likeness of cheekbones,
> smell the same breath.

My husband, I want to love you by habit,
to find in our fingernails the same moons,

but tonight you are a foreigner in my bed –
even the texture of your skin is unknown,

the shells of your ears from another ocean,
and your lips the soft duff of an old forest

I am entering as if for the first time:

> *a brilliant cathedral of quiet,*
> *only the shadow*
>
> *of a coasting owl.*

Scotch Broom

Fifty years ago wild asparagus grew by the Hudson
and watercress rippled in Warburton's brook.
Fifty years ago I didn't love you.
You were a little boy on the west side of the country,
curly hair cut close to your skull.
Meticulous and curious,
you were training to be a good lover.

On the east side of the country I was waiting
for the Russians
and didn't expect to grow up;
my baby sister thought I could save her.
My parents were grown-ups and had no lives,
but I wept for my dog who couldn't see colors.

Now I am walking on your side of the country,
an invader
like these yellow clumps of scotch broom.
On a gravel road in the old Tillamook Burn,
I step over blackberry canes and beer cans.

From this high clearing, I almost see the coast.
Clouds lie on the humps of Saddle Mountain
as on the back of a Bactrian camel,
and the long caravan of our lives

seems small and far off, and only when I listen hard
do I hear the bells. They are shaped like pods
or the cups of flowers.

4. The Spirit of the World

The Barn of Desolation: November

The donkey's eyelashes lay on my cheek like wet lace;
I was, to the donkey, a voluntary comrade in grief.

When the compliant bailiff, that minor occupant of shoes,
slid open the wide door in a rustle of straw and duplicate forms,

I asked for all the second pages, I begged for the yellow copies,
I insisted on signed promises.

Window squares shone on blue snow: trampled and tracked,
tracked and trammeled, nothing simple, not one thing.

Even an old donkey remembers the taste of windfall apples;
my mouth is full of yellow jackets, my stung lips burn with kisses.

The child who came with a sputtering candle has snuffed it
out in the snow.

Deeded Rights

Here at the sacred fishing grounds
on the banks of the Klickitat,

turnbuckles into the rocks, brown glass
on a flimsy platform suspended over

the rush of the narrows, stinking salmon
on the gravel road, fly-bit guts, fish scales

like flaked mica, the duct-taped poles
with nets, purple grass in the meadow,

ripped blue plastic, my native dreams
gone blank as rainwater puddled in rocks,

this slant trailer with smashed windows
and two wet mattresses. Tinfoil packets

I thought were condoms turn out to be
taco sauce. *Pristine* and *holy*

so seldom the same.

Calendar Girl

They have taken their paring knives
to her flesh:

this red chunk is quivering on Monday,
that one on Thursday.

They have lopped off a couple of fingers
to plug up the holes in Tuesday.

Her silk-shod right foot tromps onto Saturday,
her bare left foot slips on Sunday;

one eyeball on Wednesday night, the other
at the grocery on Friday morning.

Every day of the week, her breasts
are busy ironing clothes;

they never finish.
The metal ironing board stands

erect in her vagina,
no steam left in the iron.

A Short History of Civilization

When we danced in the mouth of the cave,
we lit a blue lamp the exact shape of twilight:
its shade was punctured with cut-outs of dark birds.

Our arms lost language; lips forgot how to listen.
Our shadows thickened. Yes, we inhabited rock,
but a lush assurance of trees wanted to possess us

entirely, syrup of life rising up through our limbs,
our heads in bloom. Meantime we were mastering
methodologies of evil: To beat a snake with a stick.

To disavow human affection. To wad black powder
into the long gun, like ramming your thumb so far
down your throat that you jam your own heart.

In this Time of War,

I've rummaged too long in my dresser drawers sniffing
at dead sachets. Even the rose petals are scraps

of paper with no names written down. So how
must I dress myself to walk about upon

this reddened earth? Today I will wear my snazzy
new panties of snake skin, those cool translucent scales

that slither in only one direction, up.
Never to droop or gather about my ankles.

I once knew a woman who lived through the London Blitz,
and her knickers were stitched from German parachute silk –

all the elastic had gone to the army, only
a safety pin to hold her homemade panties

up; she stood on the platform at Waterloo Station
where a long troop train chugged in with the wounded,

and just as her right hand ascended to her forehead
in quick salute, her slippery silk panties descended

and puddled over her sensible shoes, and she stepped
right out of them and kept on walking,

leaving all that tender and airworthy silk
under the crooked and shell-shocked wheels

of the gurney, so many gurneys.

Dancing on the Berlin Wall

Troy torches Dresden. In Rome,
in Babylon, in Gettysburg,
they slaughter.

I hid in the stacks reading Marx,
bombs ticking overhead.
Where is she, my little sister?

Then, on a night in November,
Decade Five of the Cold War,
my fingers unknotted like barbed wire.

Consider the fireproof thumbs
of mothers
who murder for babes.

I raised two kids beyond my strength
and fed them turnips. Was this
heroic?

I suck gasoline from my finger,
and my tongue flames.
I believe in apes and angels.

High on the Wall, angels prance.
But my old father folds his arms,
those mute and skeptic wings

that cannot dance or fly,
whose late white feathers
hum and sing.

The Angels of New Orleans

There is an angel for every minute
but they are all looking away.

There was a twirling angel
riding the eye of the hurricane.

There is an angel for the gash
in the wall of the seventeenth street canal.

There is an angel for the infant
born on concrete between stadium seats.

There is an angel for the dead man
with his head slumped in a lawn chair.

There is another angel for the tarp
nobody spread over his body.

The multiple angels for the government
are busy watching golf on cable.

There is an angel for the old woman
floating face down under her rafters.

There is a special angel for her dog
who howls at the receding helicopter.

There are almost enough angels
that they might have made a difference.

A picayune angel here in Portland
is paying attention. She slaps my face.

She twists the wrist writing my check.
She says, *Angels forbid the word* ***deserve.***

She says, *Swallow the brown water,*
the mud, the rot, the excrement,

the heavenly shimmer of gasoline.
Now go downtown and feed your own.

Big Dipper over my City

When there is urine in the public stairwell
you know somebody is alive
someone has unzipped his trousers
or squatted under her skirt
there has been water to drink from a public fountain
or else wine or the gruel of salvation
this is the urine of someone who once was diapered
and maybe even kissed on the belly

When a damp sleeping bag is spread between rows
of pruned and flat-topped municipal plane trees
whose roots poke into rubble and fish bones
and the chilly toes of the sleeper poke through
blown-out socks into shoes without laces
you know how sleep is scavenged among strangers
and the sleeper is vexed by streetlights
and linked couples trailing home

On a clear night when the dipper glows over towers
and its starry ladle dribbles equally everywhere
what you may not know is how seriously
I go about choosing one sheltered doorway
or another for curling with my dog and how
all night long no matter where I do sleep
I will be clutching in my invisible dream-hands
the dented bowl from which the dog laps water

with her thin hot tongue

Inside the Snail's Curled Shell

Precious horns of the snail, you are two slim chimneys.
The sun casts its shadow over your chitinous doorsill.

My father has bolted shut the door to his eyes.
Under this white trillium, I crouch in memoriam.

Snail, how do you mount the rungs of a licorice fern?
Teach me the right way up. Teach me the right way in.

My pinkie curls into your shell.
Snail, snail,

must I go on traveling, always hunting for the fleshy
ridge lines of home?

Somewhere to Sleep

The pick-up truck with the dog.
The dirt track that is two roads.

The spacious life where you veer
both left and right, and both

are right, and before full dark
you'll have somewhere to sleep,

and the dog slobbers your feet.
You have never been so clean.

Caring for the World

It's all right if I hold the old lady by her bony shoulders
as she hawks yellow sputum onto her jello.

It's all right if the man in the elastic truss has crusted feces
on the crease of his sunken scrotum.

It's more than all right if I walk bare-toed through the dung
in the barnyard. All day the cows have munched sunshine,

and at night, in their stanchions under the lantern,
they move rumen from one stomach to the next.

There was a raised bump on the flesh of my side
and I gave myself permission to scrape it off with my thumbnail;

it was an agreement between nail and skin, and a dot of blood
rose on my skin and dried under my fingernail.

Everything living is beautiful and ugly: the gelatinous egg sack
and the flexible, transparent quill of the squid.

After we put down our old dog, I lay on her couch inhaling
the scent of the scent of her leaked urine.

The couch was a meadow and I was a butterfly,
and over my wings the sky kept on flowing.

I am your dead dog

come home to greet you. Sunset curls into blue hills.
Out in your garden, my bones dry in our earth's crust.
That pink streak under clouds is a line where our sky

cracks. On a far planet nobody I know of grows fur.
Here is a ditty broken in two: one yip in a coat of silence.
This is the taste of erasure, my mute and nimble tongue

licking your face. It was time; I needed to leave you.
Whatever is beautiful is multiple, is what eats and shits
and breathes, is what still ***wants****. You can imagine me*

speaking in well-intoned English, if that's what you want.

The Ladylike Cough

This is the ladylike cough, discreet
in the hand or the lace hankie.

This is the cough that hates to interrupt --
it tiptoes out of the hall to wait in the lobby;
it swallows itself.

This isn't the editorial cough that poses
a wordless critique complete with the look --
you know that look,

nor coughs from my baby sister's room
where I made it my job to be certain
she breathed.

This isn't my geriatric dog gagging.

This isn't the raggedy man waiting outside
the Thriftway for change and coughing
inside the rain.

If the man and his smell step into this poem,
I'll hand him two quarters and try not to hold
my breath.

I'd like to think I'd give him this whole wedge
of sharp white cheddar and my beautiful loaf
of nine-grain bread.

I'd like to believe I'm telling you the truth

just as I'd like to believe I can't be stuck
coughing in jail or an alley or deep
in the yellow mud of a refugee camp.

Some of us are born with lace hankies.
Some of us like to think so.

Flying East for my Grandson's Birth

And I'm sailing in high silver over Pendleton and Bozeman
as you journey the last hard inches toward the sill of the pubis.

At 33,000 feet, the outside temperature, according to the screen
and these frost flowers blooming here on the window by my seat,
is minus 59 degrees Fahrenheit.

Council Bluffs and the rectangular plains marking buffalo bones
in late snow. Now the thick Mississippi twists like an umbilical,
and the cord, coiled through generations, tightens my groin.

Push, they told me, and what else could I do, my back cracking
over the rim of the world?

At the darkening edge of the continent,
she is breathing and sweating. Let somebody's cool hand
sweep damp hair from her forehead.

As I pass over Cincinnati, she is opening in waves and scarlet
birth blood is flowing through us all. East now of Pittsburgh
she is riding her moment of *I can't do this any more*, the body
almost inverting itself, and clouds rushing under my wings,
until the lift and gasp in the moving air.

Sometimes we call this
landing.

Child, I will tell you every glorious thing I know:
We are made out of dirt and water. Someday your hands
will have freckles and lines. Many cherished people
have lived and died before you.

Oh, and, child, one thing more:
this earth invents us and consorts with us willingly
only because we tell stories.

The Midwife's Trade

I am catching the babies. Clotted and slippery, they slide
down the blue thighs of the sky,

Each baby arrives with a ticket on a string.

So many babies. I stack them in cradles woven of wheat.
They breathe like the leaning of winter wheat

toward a dim horizon. Somewhere under the north quarter,
roots croon to the stars.

We are raising your babies, the wheat insists, ignorant
of threshers.

By the time these babies get old, they all will have lost
their return tickets.

So I will pull down the pull-down staircase that opens
into the sky. I will climb the ladder and hustle them up,

like luggage into an unfloored attic. There they will wait
with the spiders and silverfish

until somebody gets ready to journey again.

I am paid in barter for this job. I forget what I know
but I remember what you know.

One Theory of Composition

Here, under mossy white trunks of alders,
I am waiting for salmon to come up the creek.

In the black pools by the undercut bank,
in vaulted and shadowy passages under
hollow stumps of gigantic cedars,

I am waiting for salmon to leap over riffles.

On the damp foot trail along the creek
where ruffled mushrooms sprout under logs
in the twilight of browning sword ferns,
I am waiting,

waiting for salmon to spawn eggs from death.

In the thin anthem of Soapstone Creek,
in a night-fog of saplings where one word
contains *spirit-who-splits-around-rocks*,

I am waiting to decompose.

Soon I will type only syllables or letters.
I will say *buh* or *mmm* like an infant.
I will be as non-linguistic as a salmon.

Or like the creek,
hummmmmmmm

December Again

Flush of the snowberry bush, its multiple eyeless white skulls,
or each pinecone a file cabinet of seeds the ground squirrels
re-file, the Tualatin Valley flooded with fog, treetops rising
as stranded black islands, a new winter without our old dog,
always weather rushing to somewhere else, each snowberry
a white light in a dim day like eyes of friends, or eyes we have
closed. Even in darkness, not everything ends.

It begins,
it grows, it learns to speak. A little child got up from his nap.
Half-way down the scary stairs he announced, *I love myself.*
And don't you believe he was right to say it?

Such shameless,
shameless bliss: deft hands of the greedy squirrel, sweetness
layered in the scales of a pinecone, or sunrise as if witnessed
from inside the shell of an egg.

About the Author

Penelope Scambly Schott has worked as a donut maker in a cider mill, a home health aide, an artist's model, and, through it all, a college professor. After many years in rural New Jersey, she moved to Portland, Oregon where she writes, paints, hikes, and spoils her husband and her current dog more completely than it would have been safe to spoil her children.

She has published a novel, four chapbooks, and five full-length books of poetry, including three historical narratives and two collections. These are *The Perfect Mother* (Violet Reed Hass Prize, 1994), *Penelope: The Story of Half-Scalped Woman* (1999), *The Pest Maiden: A Story of Lobotomy* (2004), *Baiting the Void* (Orphic Prize, 2005), and *A Is for Anne: Mistress Hutchinson Disturbs the Commonwealth* (2007).

She is a member of three poetry group, Pearls, Portlandia, and The Cool Women Poets of New Jersey, and her poetry is included on the new CD *The Cool Women Collect Themselves*. When she lived in New Jersey, she was awarded four fellowships by the New Jersey Council on the Arts, and she has done residencies at The Fine Arts Workcenter in Provincetown, Massachusetts, The Vermont Studio Center, and most recently The Wurlitzer Foundation in Taos, New Mexico where an argumentative magpie insisted on dictating poems to her. In an ongoing effort to be agreeable, she wrote them down.